News Flash #710
A 30-Day Journal

Pearl and Johnny Williams

Unless otherwise indicated, all scripture references are from
King James Version (KJV)
Amplified Version (AMP)

News Flash #710: A 30-Day Journal
© March 2021 Pearl and Johnny Williams
ISBN# 978-1-953526-06-9

All rights reserved under International copyright law. This book or parts of thereof may not be reproduced in any form, stored in a retrieval system, or transmitted in any form by any means; electronic, mechanical, photocopy, recording, or otherwise without prior written permission of the publisher or author, except as provided by United States of America copyright.

Published by TaylorMade Publishing
Jacksonville, FL
www.TaylorMadePublishingFL.com
(904) 323-1334

Table of Contents

Dedication i
Purpose ii
Day 1: Nothing But The Blood! 1
Day 2: Are You Listening? 3
Day 3: God Is Good! 6
Day 4: You Can Trust God 9
Day 5: What A Friend We Have In Jesus! 11
Day 6: What's The Rush? 14
Day 7: Love Never Fails 16
Day 8: Stay Hopeful 19
Day 9: It's Time To Wake Up, Get Up, And Return To God! 22
Day 10: Out With The Old And Begin With A New 24
Day 11: It's Time To Rejoice! 27
Day 12: The Bible 29
Day 13: The God-Kind 31
Day 14: The Power of Prayer 33
Day 15: The Spoken Word 35
Day 16: Let's Get Dressed 38
Day 17: Did I Say That? 41
Day 18: Reconciliation 43
Day 19: Faith Is Always Now! 46
Day 20: "This Year" 49
Day 21: The Ministry of After 52
Day 22: It Is Finished 55
Day 23: I Am Blessed 57
Day 24: Doing The Right Thing With A Made-Up Mind 60
Day 25: Churches Part 1 63
Day 26: Churches Part 2 66
Day 27: The Dry Spell Is Over! 69
Day 28: Say No To Condemnation! 72
Day 29: A Sure Foundation 75
Day 30: Get The Word On It! 78
News Flash # 710 Views & Expressions 81
Poem: Jesus Makes Everything All Right 83
About the Authors 84

Dedication

To the late Raymond Lee Moore,

On May 7, 1998, my youngest brother, Raymond Lee Moore, departed from us to spend eternity with the Lord. His departure at the age of 27 was caused by complications of sickle cell disease. His transition took place in hospital room number 710. A great host of friends and loved ones lined the hallways outside of Raymond's room. We love him and miss him, yet we all realized on that day, Raymond had a divine appointment with God.

We found comfort in knowing that for those who are in Christ *"...to be absent from the body is to be present with the Lord."* (2 Corinthians 5:8 KJV) The Spirit of God ministered to me (Pearl) through Raymond's room number the day he passed and went on to glory. This tremendous experience sparked the genesis of NEWS FLASH #710, that was printed and distributed to various households over the years. Each of these letters, written by Johnny and I, would bring to us and others the Good News of God's Kingdom through Jesus Christ His Son.

In Loving Memory

A Dear Brother and True Friend

Raymond Lee Moore
October 7, 1970 – May 7, 1998

Purpose

The message of NEWS FLASH #710 is two-fold. First, it is to bring comfort to every family that has suffered the loss of a loved one. Our sincere prayers are with you and for you. Always know that you can receive comfort from God's word. God cares and knows the pain we feel. It was God who gave us this wonderful gift of family. Let us be mindful to love, pray for, and cherish our family members because, when we do, we are making precious memories that will last forever.

Secondly, today is always a good time for us to surrender our lives, in order to receive God's gift of salvation through Jesus. It is our desire that Christians be encouraged and strengthened to live for Jesus; and if you are not a Christian, it is our sincere prayer and hope that you will want to become one, and join the saints of God as we walk in the light and love of our Lord and Savior, Jesus Christ. It is our goal in this 30-day journal to encourage, inform, and enlighten the awareness of God's love for us all.

Day 1: Nothing But The Blood!

Praise God from whom all blessings flow. We are truly a blessed and highly favored people. Whatever your needs are today, remember God is just a prayer away. Let God's wisdom and peace direct your hearts during this COVID-19 period.

Looking to God for a word of encouragement, we go to the Old Testament in the book of Exodus 12:13 (KJV), *"And the blood shall be to you for a token upon the houses where ye are: and when I see the blood, I will pass over you, and the plague shall not be upon you to destroy you, when I smite the land of Egypt."*

The blood of a lamb without blemish was to be sacrificed as a substitute for each family household for protection from the plague. From this point on, the Hebrew people would clearly understand that for them to be spared from death, an innocent life had to be sacrificed in their place.

Today, God is yet making this appeal to all people for deliverance from the bondage of sin through the blood of His Son, Jesus. We don't have to live in fear, for God is yet calling out WHEN I SEE THE BLOOD, I'LL PASS OVER! Just as the Israelites trusted God for protection and safety by being obedient to apply the blood to the door post of their houses, our obedience to accept Jesus as Lord places us under HIS PRECIOUS BLOOD COVERING!

"Trust in and rely confidently on the Lord with all your heart and do not rely on your own insight or understanding." (Proverbs 3:5 AMP) As we obey the laws of the land, let's remember to pray for everyone, especially health care workers and those in any leadership capacity.

Reflection of the Day:

Day 2: Are You Listening?

Oftentimes we are asked a question and we give a response without really hearing what was asked. How important it is that we listen and understand the question before a response is given? We began this day by asking the question, are you listening? To listen means to give close attention in order to hear; to give ear to (to understand), to hear and attend to (to obey).

In the Gospel of St. John, chapter 21:15-17 (KJV), Jesus asked Peter a question, *"...Simon, son of Jonas, lovest thou me more than these? He saith unto him, Yea, Lord; thou knowest that I love thee. He saith unto him, Feed my lambs. He saith to him again the second time, Simon, son of Jonas, lovest thou me? He saith unto him, Yea, Lord; thou knowest that I love thee. He saith unto him, Feed my sheep. He saith unto him the third time, Simon, son of Jonas, lovest thou me? Peter was grieved because he said unto him the third time, Lovest thou me? And he said unto him, Lord, thou knowest all things; thou knowest that I love thee. Jesus saith unto him, Feed my sheep."*

The first time Jesus was asking Peter, are you listening? The second time, He wanted to know, do you understand? The third time, He was asking Peter, will you obey? It is God's will and desire that His word be established in us, but we must first hear, understand, and do. Are you listening?

It is important to know what God's word says, but it is much more important to obey it. In other words, information is good, but it doesn't benefit us until we apply it, and we can't apply it if we don't understand it. Once we hear and understand what God's word says, we must take the next step and obey. Being a hearer of the Word and not a doer has no profit. But hearing and doing the word opens the door and God's blessings are sure to flow.

If you were to set a four-course meal before a starving man and all he did was say, 'Thank you, this food sure looks and smells good,' but he never ate it, what do you think would happen?

Likewise, just to say you went to church is not enough. You can see the effectiveness of time spent in church service hearing the gospel by a person's attitude and behavior in life. In other words, the preacher provides information to us, we in turn must do something with it. To those who are listening, it becomes revelation, and they apply the principles to their lives and inherit the promises.

God's word teaches us so many good things; He says "I love you. Love one another. Pray for one another. Live in peace with one another. Love your enemies, and pray for those that despitefully use you. I am the way, the truth, and the life." But are we listening?

Reflection of the Day:

Day 3: God Is Good!

Great is the Lord and He is greatly to be praised. What a privilege it is to know and serve the Lord Jesus. Our God is a merciful, gracious, and loving God. I like the way that the Psalmist makes it so clear, *"O give thanks unto the Lord; for he is good: for his mercy endureth for ever."* (Psalms 136:1 KJV) It is so good to know that we have an inexhaustible supply of God's mercy available to us. This mercy is for our growth and maturity in Him as well as the advancement of His kingdom.

The mercy of God brings us to salvation. *"It is of the Lord's mercies that we are not consumed, because his compassions fail not."* (Lamentations 3:22 KJV) Thanks be to God for His kindness and compassion, and it doesn't stop there. *"Surely goodness and mercy shall follow me all the days of my life: and I will dwell in the house of the Lord for ever."* (Psalms 23:6 KJV) People are often frightened when they encounter strange and unknown situations in their lives. Wouldn't it make you feel so much better knowing that goodness and mercy are following you all through life's journey? Hallelujah!

God loves us and it is His desire to keep us from harm. God cares for the young as well as the old and we never diminish in value to Him. We have this promise in His Word that He will never leave us or forsake us. Yes, God is truly amazing. He forgives all of our iniquities, and heals all our diseases. He has redeemed our lives from destruction and crowned us with his loving kindness and tender mercies.

As God has been faithful to redeem and bless us, we must each be faithful to praise and to serve Him. *"Oh that men would praise the LORD for his goodness, and for his wonderful works to the children of men!"* (Psalms 107:8 KJV)

NEWS FLASH #710

From childhood we are taught that when someone does something good for you, don't forget to say, 'Thank you.' When we think of all the benefits and goodness of God in our everyday lives, come on and tell the Lord THANK YOU!

Reflection of the Day:

Day 4: You Can Trust God

As we venture through life and our everyday situations, we see more and more why it is important to put our trust in God. We live in a world where we are constantly interacting with one another; we know that relationships are very important. We all need something or someone we can depend on and place our confidence in. This assured reliance on the ability, strength, and character of someone is called TRUST. It is important to understand that our trust or confidence is only as good as what it is placed in. In other words, in order for our trust to remain constant, the person or thing has to remain the same and not change.

We know that circumstances and situations change, people change, and even our positions in life change. In this changing world we can trust in an unchanging God. In Malachi 3:6a it says, *"For I am the Lord, I change not..."* and Hebrews 13:8 (KJV) says, *"Jesus Christ the same yesterday, and to day, and for ever."* We can trust, lean, and depend on God who will never change. He has been and will always remain the same forever. No matter what decisions or directions life brings your way, you can trust in God.

In Proverbs 3:5-6 (KJV) it says, *"Trust in the Lord with all thine heart; and lean not unto thine own understanding. In all thy ways acknowledge him, and he shall direct thy paths."* Even with our God given ability to reason, there are times when we can't trust ourselves. But we should always be willing to trust the instructions from God. We do this by going to God in prayer, using the Bible as our guide, and following the Holy Spirit's leading. Psalm 119:105 (KJV) says, *"Thy word is a lamp unto my feet, and a light unto my path."* John 8:12 (KJV), says, *"Then spake Jesus again unto them, saying, I am the light of the world: he that followeth me shall not walk in darkness, but shall have the light of life."* With a lamp to guide you and a clear path to follow, who wouldn't trust that?

Reflection of the Day:

Day 5: What A Friend We Have In Jesus!

It is so wonderful to have people or that special someone in your life that you can talk to. Someone who makes themselves available to listen, help, and encourage you when you need it. Someone that is not hostile but thankful. A person that is willing to share an intimate bond and commitment in a relationship that we call friendship.

A good friend has to know when to give advice and when to show compassion. In Job 6:6-7 (KJV), Job said that Eliphaz's advice was like the disgusting white of an uncooked egg. When people are going through severe trials, ill-advised counsel is as distasteful as slimy food. They may listen politely, but inside they feel like gagging. People in a hurting situation need compassion more than advice. A good friend will know which is best in most situations.

God constantly gives us comfort, compassion, and advice through His Word. There is a friend that sticks closer than a brother, and in Him we can put all of our trust. **What a friend we have in Jesus!** Sometimes in life our natural friends tend to leave us or evade us, but Jesus said He would never leave us nor forsake us.

He tells us to cast all of our care upon Him for He cares for us. (I Peter 5:7.) In St John 15:13-15 (KJV) Jesus said, *"Greater love hath no man than this, that a man lay down his life for his friends. Ye are my friends, if ye do whatsoever I command you. Henceforth I call you not servants; for the servant knoweth not what his lord doeth: but I have called you friends; for all things that I have heard of my Father I have made known unto you."*

Jesus has given us an example of what friendship should be like. He gave his life for us that we may have life more abundantly. Oh, how this inspires us to be the best friend that we can be.

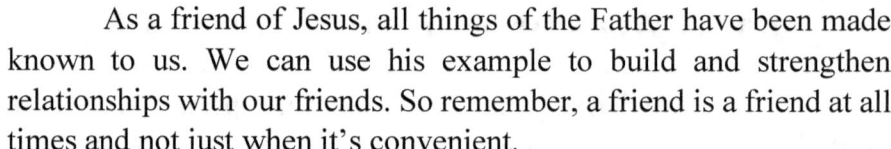

    As a friend of Jesus, all things of the Father have been made known to us. We can use his example to build and strengthen relationships with our friends. So remember, a friend is a friend at all times and not just when it's convenient.

Reflection of the Day:

Day 6: What's The Rush?

Praise God for the opportunity and blessing to live, love, and fulfill our God given purpose as we look to Him. When I think back, it seems like time is moving so fast. With all the adjustments and changes over the years, it has truly been one learning experience after another. People transitioning from one job to another, one city to another, and others transitioned to glory! Thank God for our trust and confident hope in Him! Amen!

As we prepare ourselves for the days ahead, consider the effects of overload that lead to racing against the clock. Understanding that some things have a time period attached to them, procrastination is not wise. We are referring to being R-U-S-H-E-D, not being in the present moment. Philippians 4:6 (AMP) states, *"Do not be anxious or worried about anything, but in everything [every circumstance and situation] by prayer and petition with thanksgiving, continue to make your [specific] requests known to God."* When we rush, we are putting ourselves in a place of opposition. This creates a type of consciousness that appears when we are feeling worried or anxious.

Racing through life can be draining and exhausting and produces a feeling of lack. Let's slow down and learn to be attentive. Psalm 46:10 (AMP), says, *"Be still and know (recognize, understand) that I am God. I will be exalted among the nations! I will be exalted in the earth."*

Let's learn to be present and aware of all things. Don't be like the person who missed their package delivery because they weren't home. Cherish every moment in life. Let go of the **R-U-S-H** and experience a higher connection with joy, peace, and love. After all, God has a delivery for you, but you must be **P-R-E-S-E-N-T** to receive it.

NEWS FLASH #710

Reflection of the Day:

Day 7: Love Never Fails

God has blessed us through another year, and for that we say, "LORD, WE THANK YOU!" We spend a lot of time on New Year resolutions that we usually abandon within three or four months. They usually focus on things we need to stop doing versus things we need to start doing. Let's discard our list of resolutions this year and focus on showing more LOVE towards others. If we are concerned about the negative things in our lives, Proverbs 10:12 states that "love covers all sins" as well as faults, flaws, and bad habits. God is Love. (1 John 4:8)

In order to love others, we must first love God. Let us demonstrate our love to others as God has demonstrated his love to us. Paul states in Romans 14:19 (KJV), *"Let us therefore follow after the things which makes for peace, and things wherewith one may edify or build up another."* Our hearts should be concerned with encouraging and building up others.

Romans 15:3 (AMP) shows, *"For even Christ did not please himself..."* He came to serve others. Just as Christ knew that in serving others, His own assurance rested in the Father, so shall we be confident that our assurance rests in our Lord and Savior, Jesus Christ. So, instead of wasting our precious time on improving our lives through New Year resolutions, let us allow God's love for us and our love for others to bring about positive changes in our lives this year. "LOVE never fails"

"Finally, brethren, whatsoever things are true, whatsoever things are honest, whatsoever things are just, whatsoever things are pure, whatsoever things are lovely, whatsoever things are of good report; if there be any virtue, and if there be any praise, think on these things." (Philippians 4:8 KJV)

L O V E is: **L**etting **O**ur **V**oice **E**cho Father God.

L O V E is: **L**iving **O**ne **V**ision **E**very day that glorifies and pleases God.

L O V E is: **L**oving **O**thers **V**erses **E**nvy.

NEWS FLASH #710

Reflection of the Day:

Day 8: Stay Hopeful

During the election year of 2008, the nation went through many changes. There was one new beginning after another. One in particular marks a new era in the history of the United States. On November 4, 2008, our 44th president was the first African American to be elected to this office. This election of Barack Obama as President ended one era and began another. Where one thing ends, another begins.

In 2008, we experienced many new beginnings; some were of a personal nature and others on a much broader scale. We celebrated new open doors of opportunity with each of you. We also remembered and prayed for those of you who suffered loss. The good brought tears of gladness and the losses brought tears of sadness. That year alone, our economic system went through dramatic and devastating changes. At the year's end and 2009's beginning, we hoped and looked forward to a brighter future.

As believers in Christ, no matter what takes place in the world around us, we must keep in mind this truth from God's word, *"If in this life only we have hope in Christ, we are of all men most miserable."* (I Corinthians 15:19 KJV) We have a sure promise from God for our lives now, and in that which is to come. In other words the end is yet the beginning.

Revelations 21:3—5 (KJV) explains it this way, *"And I heard a great voice out of heaven saying, Behold, the tabernacle of God is with men, and he will dwell with them, and they shall be his people, and God Himself shall be with them, and be their God. And God shall wipe away all tears from their eyes; and there shall be no more death, neither sorrow, nor crying, neither shall there be any more pain: for the former things are passed away. ...Behold, I make all things new..."* We serve an eternal God.

Revelations 22:13 (AMP), *"I am the Alpha and Omega, the Beginning and the End, the First and the Last."* Trust God's love while you fulfill your purpose on earth in preparation for eternity.

THANK GOD FOR NEW LIFE IN "JESUS" Hallelujah!!

H-ow **O**-ne **P**-erson **E**-merges

HOPE!

Reflection of the Day:

NEWS FLASH #710

Day 9: It's Time To Wake Up, Get Up, And Return To God!

Praise God from Whom all blessings flow. We give honor to God through his son Jesus who has secured our victory and has given us access through faith to the precious promises of God. We, as God's representatives in this earthly realm, have been entrusted with the ministry of reconciliation.

"But all these things are from God, who reconciled us to Himself through Christ [making us acceptable to Him] and gave us the ministry of reconciliation [so that by our example we might bring others to Him], that is, that God was in Christ reconciling the world to Himself, not counting people's sins against them [but canceling them]. And He has committed to us the message of reconciliation [that is, restoration to favor with God]." II Corinthians 5:18-21 (AMP)

Reconciliation is the end of the estrangement, caused by original sin, between God and humanity. It means to restore, to bring back, to mend and put back in friendly relationship. God, who is love, is seeking to restore relationships with all who will come to Him in faith.

John 3:16-17 (AMP), *"For God so [greatly] loved and dearly prized the world, that He [even] gave His [One and] only begotten Son, so that whoever believes and trusts in Him [as Savior] shall not perish, but have eternal life. For God did not send the Son into the world to judge and condemn the world [that is, to initiate the final judgment of the world], but that the world might be saved through Him."* Salvation comes by accepting Jesus, therefore reconciling us back to God our creator. The streetlight is about to come on and it's time to come home!

Reflection of the Day:

Day 10: Out With The Old And Begin With A New

Today is a good day to place our focus on planning for eternity, by doing God's will as we go forward in this life. Every day is truly a day of thanksgiving because of all of the wonderful works of God in our lives. God has been there for us in our trying and difficult times. He has put people in our lives to encourage and help us. God's word is reliable and has remained true in every situation. His precious Holy Spirit has been our guiding strength and counselor.

It is because God loved us so much that He gave his son Jesus, and through us his children, He is still giving. Yes, just lending a helping hand is God's plan. When we allow the word of God to minister to our hearts about the changes needed in our lives, He whispers resolutions that turn into solutions.

You would be surprised at the service you render to God when you render acts of kindness and help to others. Many times we overlook the fact that by helping others we are indeed serving God. In Matthew 25:34-40 (KJV), Jesus says, *"Then shall the King say unto them on his right hand, Come, ye blessed of my Father, inherit the kingdom prepared for you from the foundation of the world: For I was an hungred, and ye gave me meat: I was thirsty, and ye gave me drink: I was a stranger, and ye took me in: Naked, and ye clothed me: I was sick, and ye visited me: I was in prison, and ye came unto me. Then shall the righteous answer him, saying, Lord, when saw we thee an hungred, and fed thee? or thirsty, and gave thee drink? When saw we thee a stranger, and took thee in? or naked, and clothed thee? Or when saw we thee sick, or in prison, and came unto thee? And the King shall answer and say unto them, Verily I say unto you, Inasmuch as ye have done it unto one of the least of these my brethren, ye have done it unto me."*

NEWS FLASH #710

No act of kindness is too small when meeting the needs of others. We all have this God given ability to do well toward others. Realizing that we have what it takes, let us use what we have to be a blessing to others and bring Glory to God. Galatians 6:7 tells us, *"Be not deceived; God is not mocked: for whatsoever a man soweth, that shall he also reap."* People who sow love and kindness into the lives of others cannot keep it for themselves.

NEWS FLASH #710

Reflection of the Day:

NEWS FLASH #710

Day 11: It's Time To Rejoice!

There is no God like our God! Jesus is King of kings and Lord of lords. He is the Alpha and Omega, the first and the last, the beginning and the end. He is the Bishop of souls, the bright and morning star. He is the Light of the world. Jesus is a mind regulator, a heart fixer, and a lawyer in the court room. He is our provider and sustainer. He is our Lord and Savior. His precious blood has redeemed us. We walk in victory; we are blessed and highly favored. IT'S TIME TO REJOICE! HALLELUJAH! Somebody tell God thank you!

God is our deliverer, and we thank Him for the victory. In Psalms 18:2 (KJV), David declares, *"The Lord is my rock, my fortress, and the One who rescues me; My God, my rock and strength in whom I trust and take refuge; My shield, and the horn of my salvation, my high tower—my stronghold."* IT'S TIME TO REJOICE! Come on and bless His holy name!

Our God is a good God. Psalms 103:1-6 says, *"Bless the Lord, O my soul: and **all** that is within me, bless his holy name. Bless the Lord, O my soul, and forget not **all** his benefits: Who forgiveth **all** thine iniquities; who healeth **all** thy diseases; Who redeemeth thy life from destruction; who crowneth thee with lovingkindness and tender mercies; Who satisfieth thy mouth with good things; so that thy youth is renewed like the eagle's. The Lord executeth righteousness and judgment for **all** that are oppressed."* And what comes after **ALL**? I tell you, **IT'S TIME TO REJOICE!** Don't wait or even hesitate. Come on in where the table is spread, and the feast of God's blessings is going on. God is listening; will you say YES to Jesus? When you do, there are times of rejoicing waiting just for you! GOD LOVED US; JESUS DIED TO SAVE US!

NEWS FLASH #710

Reflection of the Day:

Day 12: The Bible

I can remember the lyrics to the song, "Yes Jesus loves me, for the Bible tells me so." I am sure many of us can remember that song and the blessing that it has been to us. There are so many treasures in the Bible for God's people. The Bible is Holy, it is God speaking to his family of believers on earth.

2 Timothy 3:15-17 (KJV) says, *"And that from a child thou hast known the holy scriptures, which are able to make thee wise unto salvation through faith which is in Christ Jesus. All scripture is given by inspiration of God, and is profitable for doctrine, for reproof, for correction, for instruction in righteousness: That the man of God may be perfect, thoroughly furnished unto all good works."*

The Bible is **B**-basic **I**-instructions **B**-before **L**-leaving **E**-earth.
- Number one, the Bible gives us understanding in how to receive salvation through faith in Jesus Christ.
- Number two, the Bible is God speaking to us to teach us, guide us, and correct us into right behavior with Him as well as others.
- Number three, the Bible is to make us complete, proficient, and equipped to live out our God given purpose in life.
- Number four, the Bible is our Global Positioning System (GPS), to direct our steps, answer our questions, and prepare us for eternity with God.

The Bible is the most important book any person will ever read. God's word has so much in it for all who will believe and receive it. Proverbs 3:2 (KJV) lets us know, *"For length of days, and long life, and peace, shall they add to thee."*

NEWS FLASH #710

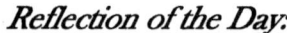

Reflection of the Day:

NEWS FLASH #710

Day 13: The God-Kind

The answer to so many problems in life is found in this one statement, 'God's love never fails!' If we learn to walk in love, we are sure not to fail. I am talking about divine love, not human love, but God's love in us. God has made his love available to us and it begins with salvation (see Romans 10:9-10).

Once we have surrendered our lives to God, we are born again. In other words, a new birth has taken place. The next question you might ask is, just how will I know that I have received salvation? According to the Bible, this happens by faith.

When we repent of sin, believe, and confess Jesus Christ as our Lord and Savior, it is done. The Bible also says, *"And hope maketh not ashamed; because the love of God is shed abroad in our hearts by the Holy Ghost which is given unto us."* (Romans 5:5 KJV). In the new birth process, God's abundant love has been poured out within our hearts through his Holy Spirit which has been given to us.

We don't have to pray for love, because God has already given every believer a measure of the **God-kind** of love, just as He has given the **God-kind** of faith. Feeding on the word of God and applying what the word tells us in our everyday lives, is how we increase the **God-kind** of way to live and operate.

Love is the key that unlocks any door, solves any problem, conquers any situation but, we must be willing and obedient to address them with the **God-kind** of answers. 1 John 4:4 (KJV) states, *"Ye are of God, little children, and have overcome them: because greater is he that is in you, than he that is in the world."* Let's live the love life, and spread it all around. Then others will see and benefit from the lives we live, as we bring glory to our heavenly father.

NEWS FLASH #710

Reflection of the Day:

Day 14: The Power of Prayer

What a wonderful and powerful avenue of communication we have been given as children of God. No matter where we are or what we are doing we have continual and total access to God through prayer. There are many benefits to prayer Luke18:1 (KJV), it says, *"And he spake a parable unto them to this end, that men ought always to pray, and not to faint."*

Jesus was telling a parable to his disciples to make the point that at all times, they are to pray and not give up and lose heart. Prayer is a strengthener and a keeper that helps us to continue on in life. In Matthew 21:22 (KJV) it says, *"And all things, whatsoever ye shall ask in prayer, believing, ye shall receive."* Jesus was telling us that as we pray, we should believe in order to receive what we are asking for. This is of course according to His word and will. There is so much power in prayer.

When someone needs help we can pray for them. James 5:15-16 (KJV) says, *"And the prayer of faith shall save the sick, and the Lord shall raise him up; and if he have committed sins, they shall be forgiven him. Confess your faults one to another, and pray one for another, that ye may be healed. The effectual fervent prayer of a righteous man availeth much."* When we pray in faith, God hears, forgives, and heals those we are praying for. This heartfelt and persistent prayer from a righteous person is made effective when God answers our prayers.

For the children of God, prayer is essential. In reference to the cross, the vertical line represents our communication and relationship with God. The horizontal line represents our communication and relationship with mankind. Communication brings intimacy to a relationship and gives it strength. So does the power of prayer.

PRAYER is
P-power **R**-regularly **A**-available **Y**-yielding **E**-eternal **R**-rewards

NEWS FLASH #710

Reflection of the Day:

Day 15: The Spoken Word

Because we are made in the image of God, we can be referred to as His imagers. God is truly amazing. God is sovereign, which means that He, as the creator of heaven and earth, has the absolute right and full authority to do or allow whatever He desires. It means that God answers to no one.

When God, who is a spirit, created the heavens and the earth, He spoke them into existence. Genesis 1:3, 6, 9, and 11 (KJV). *"And God said, Let there be light: and there was light. And God said, Let there be a firmament in the midst of the waters, and let it divide the waters from the waters. And God said, Let the waters under the heaven be gathered together unto one place, and let the dry land appear: and it was so."* As you can see from the scriptures, when God wanted something to happen, He spoke, and it came to pass. As imagers of God, we have also been given this ability. As "Speaking Spirits," we too have creative power in our speech. Let us look at one example of how this works.

In Matthew 17:18-21(KJV), *"Jesus was giving instructions to his disciples, And Jesus rebuked the devil; and he departed out of him: and the child was cured from that very hour. Then came the disciples to Jesus apart, and said, Why could not we cast him out? And Jesus said unto them, Because of your unbelief: for verily I say unto you, If ye have faith as a grain of mustard seed, ye shall say unto this mountain, Remove hence to yonder place; and it shall remove; and nothing shall be impossible unto you. Howbeit this kind goeth not out but by prayer and fasting."*

The very first requirement is faith. Romans 10:17 (KJV) says, *"So then faith cometh by hearing, and hearing by the word of God."* Faith comes as we read, listen to, or hear God's holy word. Faith believes what God said.

Next, by speaking God's word to the mountain, which is the circumstance or situation, what God's word says will come to pass. Nothing will be impossible as we yield ourselves to God we draw closer to Him.

Reflection of the Day:

NEWS FLASH #710

Day 16: Let's Get Dressed

Every day, we are confronted by various circumstances that determine the way we dress. It may be the weather conditions or preparations to go to a particular event. These are all natural and necessary. Today we are putting on the spiritual armour of God!

Ephesians 6:11-17 (KJV) tells us the reason for this spiritual attire, *"Put on the whole armour of God, that ye may be able to stand against the wiles of the devil. For we wrestle not against flesh and blood, but against principalities, against powers, against the rulers of the darkness of this world, against spiritual wickedness in high places. Wherefore take unto you the whole armour of God, that ye may be able to withstand in the evil day, and having done all, to stand. Stand therefore, having your loins girt about with truth, and having on the breastplate of righteousness; And your feet shod with the preparation of the gospel of peace; Above all, taking the shield of faith, wherewith ye shall be able to quench all the fiery darts of the wicked. And take the helmet of salvation, and the sword of the Spirit, which is the word of God:"*

This spiritual attire is put on to equip us against the attacks, schemes, and strategies of the devil. As children of God's family, our Father God wants us to understand this armour.

1. **Loins Girt about with Truth**: Jesus; the manifested word of God is truth (John14:6; 17:17). As believers we experience God's truth. Satan fights with lies. We must speak the truth at all times.
2. **Breastplate of Righteousness:** God's approval and right standing with Him. (2 Corinthians 5:21). The breastplate protects our hearts against Satan's attacks on our emotions, self-worth, and trust in God.
3. **Feet Shod with the Preparation of the Gospel of Peace:** Readiness to spread the good news (John 14:27). Motivated by

God, no matter where we are, to proclaim the true peace that is only available in Him.

4. **The Shield of Faith:** Protects us from the enemy's attacks of insults, setbacks, and temptations (Hebrews 11:6). All Christians have been given a measure of faith (Romans12:3b).
5. **The Helmet of Salvation:** The helmet protects our minds and keeps us from doubting God's love for us. (John 3:16). When a person says, "I don't feel saved" that person has allowed doubt to enter their mind.
6. **The Sword of The Spirit:** Which is the word of God. It is the only offensive weapon in this armour (John 6:63). The believer is to verbally cast out and bind the works of Satan (John14:12-14).

Victory comes when we speak God's word!

Reflection of the Day:

Day 17: Did I Say That?

We are made in the image of God, the only sovereign Spirit being in our universe, Who spoke creation into existence. Therefore, we too have creative power in our speech. It is so important that we say what we mean and mean what we say. Too often, we hear people ask the question, '**Did I say that?**' or 'That's not what I meant to say.' Have you ever said something that you wish you hadn't? I am sure we can all relate to this. One thing about a word, once it is spoken, it can't be taken back. Even asking for forgiveness won't change the fact of what has been spoken.

In Mark 11:21-23 (KJV) Jesus is teaching his disciples about the power of speech that they possess. *"And Peter calling to remembrance saith unto him, Master, behold, the fig tree which thou cursedst is withered away. And Jesus answering saith unto them, Have faith in God. For verily I say unto you, That whosoever shall say unto this mountain, Be thou removed, and be thou cast into the sea; and shall not doubt in his heart, but shall believe that those things which he saith shall come to pass; he shall have whatsoever he saith."* It is important to note that when Jesus spoke, it caused something to manifest. As imagers of God, when we say something, we should expect to see something.

If you are not seeing the results you desire for your life, check out what you've been saying. For example, if you need healing in your body, don't keep saying, 'I always get sick this time of year,' or 'I don't think I will ever get better.' Stating the way you feel will not change your situation. You should always believe God's word for your healing. God said that His word would not return to Him void. When we say what God says, we will get results. Getting rid of what you don't want, by replacing it with what you desire, can be as simple as the question we ask, '**Did I say that?**'

NEWS FLASH #710

Reflection of the Day:

Day 18: Reconciliation

Reconciliation with God begins with His Will, His Word, and His Way of living. It ends the estrangement from God that was caused by the original sin between God and humanity. Romans 3:10, 23 (KJV) states, *"As it is written, There is none righteous, no, not one. For all have sinned, and come short of the glory of God."*

Reconciliation is the saving grace of God, through Jesus, that is extended to humanity, causing them to be in right standing with Him. John 17:3 states, *"And this is life eternal, that they might know thee the only true God, and Jesus Christ, whom thou hast sent."*

God's Will is for us to live with Him throughout eternity. John 3:15-17 (KJV) states, *"That whosoever believeth in him should not perish, but have eternal life. For God so loved the world, that he gave his only begotten Son, that whosoever believeth in him should not perish, but have everlasting life. For God sent not his Son into the world to condemn the world; but that the world through him might be saved."* This is God's Will for humanity.

God's Word is the light and life of humanity. John 1:1-2 (KJV) states, *"In the beginning was the Word, and the Word was with God, and the Word was God. The same was in the beginning with God."* The anointed Jesus was coexisting with God in the beginning. John 1:14 (KJV) states, *"And the Word was made flesh, and dwelt among us, (and we beheld his glory, the glory as of the only begotten of the Father,) full of grace and truth."* Jesus Christ is the manifested Word of God. That is why the written word is so powerful when spoken in faith.

God's Way to reconciliation is through Jesus. John 14:6 (KJV) says, *"Jesus saith unto him, I am the way, the truth, and the life: no man cometh unto the Father, but by me."* In 2 Corinthians

5:19 (KJV) it states, *"To wit, that God was in Christ, reconciling the world unto himself, not imputing their trespasses unto them; and hath committed unto us the word of reconciliation."* That is why the gospel message is preached, that whosoever might believe and receive forgiveness of sin shall receive the free gift of eternal life through the death, burial, and resurrection of Jesus Christ.

Reflection of the Day:

NEWS FLASH #710

Day 19: Faith Is Always Now!

Faith is always in the present tense; therefore faith is always now! If a person had faith, that was good, but when believing God for a now situation it requires faith for the present. In Hebrews 11:1 (AMP) it says, *"Now faith is the assurance (title deed, confirmation) of things hoped for (divinely guaranteed), and the evidence of things not seen [the conviction of their reality—faith comprehends as fact what cannot be experienced by the physical senses]."* Faith believes you have what you ask for before you see it manifested.

Faith is God's method of operation. By faith, God created. By faith, God sent His word to heal. By faith, we received salvation. Faith is how God functions. Hebrews 11:6 (KJV) states, *"But without faith it is impossible to please him: for he that cometh to God must believe that he is, and that he is a rewarder of them that diligently seek him."* Faith is to be developed. The more we use our faith, the closer it brings us to God. Faith is the avenue that brings the unseen on the scene.

This reminds me of a play in a football game where the quarterback throws the ball down the field. Right before he throws, one of his. teammates runs ahead of him in anticipation that he will be in position down field to catch it. This person is called a receiver. Just like this receiver, we must use our faith to receive from God. This requires corresponding action on our part.

Confident expectation of our abiding trust in God and His promises, is our now faith. As children of God, we have an open door to receive all of the benefits that are listed in the Bible. Father God is a loving gift giver. Hebrews the eleventh chapter lists a few examples of the precious promises received by faith.

NEWS FLASH #710

In Luke 18:8b (KJV), Jesus asked a question, *"...when the Son of man cometh, shall he find faith on the earth?"* In other words, an audience with Jesus requires "NOW" faith! NOW faith is the hand that receives all that God gives!

Reflection of the Day:

Day 20: "This Year"

When we look back on the years that have passed, there are certain ones that stand out more so than others, like the year we were born, or the year we graduated high school. These years are usually marked by specific memorable moments. They may spark emotions of joy, laughter or even sadness. The year 2020 was not only remembered because it was the beginning of a new decade, but for so many other reasons.

The **"This Year"** experience in 2020, where COVID-19 brought about isolation, loss, uncertainty, death, division, and so much more, was unlike anything that we have ever experienced. It tested our very existence. It not only unveiled what was in our atmosphere, but also what was in our hearts. The hearts of so many began to cry out "Lord Help Us."

That invitation for help requires an open door. Revelation 3:20 (KJV) states, *"Behold, I stand at the door, and knock: if any man hear my voice, and open the door, I will come in to him, and will sup with him, and he with me."* When we open the door to God, He will come in to help and restore.

In your **"This Year"** experience, no matter what year it may be, stay open to God. Close off negative and evil influence. Get rid of unbelief and worry by trusting, leaning, and depending on God. Pray and receive God's promises daily.

Let us pray:
Father God in the name of your son Jesus, we come before you in our **"This Year"** experiences. Thank you, Father God, for being the author and finisher of our faith. Thank You, for lifting up every hung down head. Thank You, for healing the sick and comforting the bereaved. We yield ourselves to Your direction and

NEWS FLASH #710

wisdom for our lives. Thank You, for being our helper, our healer, and our deliverer. Thank you, Father God, for safety and protection. Thank You, for meeting all of our needs according to Your riches in glory. Thank You, for strength and peace. Father we thank You, for ears to hear what Your spirit is saying to Your people in this hour. Thank You, for the authority that we have in You. We cancel every wicked and demonic plan over our lives; we plead THE BLOOD OF JESUS! Father, Your kingdom come, and Your will be done in this earthly realm. Father, whatever we fail in asking, we ask that you fail not in giving. In Jesus name we pray! Amen.

NEWS FLASH #710

Reflection of the Day:

Day 21: The Ministry of After

Considering the various plights of life and our God given ability to work through them, they usually fight against our spiritual convictions. They might come from pressure, persecution, false teachers, and even worldliness. By holding on to God's truth concerning our faith and what we believe, we are able to stand.

We refer to this working confidence and trust in God as **"The Ministry of After."** The word "Ministry" being acts of Christian worship, service, and responsibilities to God and others. These acts not only bring glory to God, but cause others to benefit and be blessed when we do them.

The word "After" means later, subsequent to the time when! It is after you have gone through, after the struggle, after you have suffered that God carries out His plan through you. A good example is Joseph of the Bible, starting in the book of Genesis chapters 37-50.

After Joseph had a dream, he was put into a pit. He was then sold into slavery and placed in prison before becoming ruler over the land of Egypt. Joseph, a well-established man of great faith and trust in God, is now in position to be a blessing to all of God's people. After Daniel was thrown in the lions' den, the king made a decree that everyone in his kingdom would fear and tremble before the God of Daniel who is the living God!

In 1 Peter 5:10 (KJV) it says, *"But the God of all grace, who hath called us unto his eternal glory by Christ Jesus, after that ye have suffered a while, make you perfect, stablish, strengthen, settle you."* God is encouraging believers to trust Him by receiving and applying His grace when suffering. It is through obedience that we obtain perfection, become established and securely grounded, strengthened, and settled in our faith.

NEWS FLASH #710

The trying and testing of our faith are the building blocks of the Christian character. The depth of our character is known by how we react under pressure. Psalms 34:19 (KJV) states, *"Many are the afflictions of the righteous: but the Lord delivereth him out of them all."* Instead of complaining about our struggles, let us see them as opportunities for growth as we praise and glorify God.

NEWS FLASH #710

Reflection of the Day:

Day 22: It Is Finished

Our focus thought for today is found in the gospel of John 19:30 (KJV), *"When Jesus therefore had received the vinegar, he said, It is finished: and he bowed his head, and gave up the ghost."* Here in this verse of scripture are found the greatest words that any person could ever hear. All debts against humanity were paid and every iota of the law had been fulfilled.

God makes it very clear that He loves us and has a plan to save us from the destructive power of sin. God's desire is for each of us to experience a life that has meaning, direction, love, and peace. He makes this possible through a personal relationship with His son, Jesus Christ. As stated here in Colossians 2:13-14 (KJV) , *"And you, being dead in your sins and the uncircumcision of your flesh, hath he quickened together with him, having forgiven you all trespasses; Blotting out the handwriting of ordinances that was against us, which was contrary to us, and took it out of the way, nailing it to his cross."*

When Jesus died on the cross He took upon Himself the sin penalty of the whole human race, which was physical death. His offering of Himself was the perfect sacrifice. God accepted it as payment in full for all sin, past, present, and future for all who will believe.

To believe means that you trust and have faith in what Jesus did, and you accept it for yourself on a personal basis. It means that you accept Jesus as your Lord and Savior, by following Him with all your heart, soul, mind, and strength as long as you live. Every problem that faces humanity has been addressed by Jesus at the Cross. God is giving an invitation to:

C-come **R**-rest **O**-on **S**-salvation's **S**-sacrifice

AT THE CROSS "IT IS FINISHED"

NEWS FLASH #710

Reflection of the Day:

NEWS FLASH #710

Day 23: I Am Blessed

What exactly does it mean to be blessed? How many times have we heard the phrase **"I am blessed"** in connection with some sort of possession owned or position held? Are people blessed because of the kind of car they drive? Is it the beautiful home they live in, or is it their large bank account? Are these material things really an indication of whether a person is blessed or not? If someone does not have a lot of material possessions, does it mean that they are not blessed?

There are at least two schools of thought about what it means to be blessed. The first concept of what it means to be blessed comes from the self-interests of mankind. A person says, "if my family is well, my bank account is full and my car runs well," I am blessed. This concept is based on materialism. When we base things on what we see, it opens the door for deception. People who are blessed might think that they are not blessed if based on this concept. Luke 12:15 (KJV) states, *"And he said unto them, Take heed, and beware of covetousness: for a man's life consisteth not in the abundance of the things which he possesseth."*

The second idea of what is means to be blessed is from the word of God. In this idea, to be blessed is not determined by what we have, but who we have. It is not predicated on the things we possess, but being in right relationship with God. Psalms 1:1-3 (KJV) states, *"Blessed is the man that walketh not in the counsel of the ungodly, nor standeth in the way of sinners, nor sitteth in the seat of the scornful. But his delight is in the law of the Lord; and in his law doth he meditate day and night. And he shall be like a tree planted by the rivers of water, that bringeth forth his fruit in his season; his leaf also shall not wither; and whatsoever he doeth shall prosper."*

Following God's counsel causes us to have a blessed life. The rewards of being planted in God are stability, durability, staying refreshed, and fruitful with graceful endurance, in spite of life's circumstances. Proverbs 10:22 (KJV) states, *"The blessing of the Lord, it maketh rich, and he addeth no sorrow with it."*

The Blessing Is Being In God!

Reflection of the Day:

Day 24: Doing The Right Thing With A Made-Up Mind

Do you know what it means to do the right thing with a made-up mind? Here are some things that happen without a made-up mind. A person will say one thing and do something totally different. A person starts out strong to accomplish a goal and halfway through decides to give up, stating it's too hard.

Let's take a look at this example in Matthew 21:28-31 (KJV), *"But what think ye? A certain man had two sons; and he came to the first, and said, Son, go work to day in my vineyard. He answered and said, I will not: but afterward he repented, and went. And he came to the second, and said likewise. And he answered and said, I go, sir: and went not. Whether of them twain did the will of his father? They say unto him, The first. Jesus saith unto them, Verily I say unto you, That the publicans and the harlots go into the kingdom of God before you."*

The first son said no, I won't go, but later made up his mind to do the right thing and went. The second son said yes, I will go but did not go, because his mind was not made up to do the right thing. When people have a made-up mind to do the right thing, there will always be corresponding action to support it. They are people of integrity. They make their choices based on what is right.

Queen Esther was determined to do the right thing in spite of the opposition against her. The Persian law allowed punishment by death for entering the king's inner court without permission. Esther took that risk and went before the king to prevent the elimination of the Jewish people. Esther 4:16, (KJV) says, *"Go, gather together all the Jews that are present in Shushan, and fast ye for me, and neither eat nor drink three days, night or day: I also and my maidens will fast*

likewise; and so will I go in unto the king, which is not according to the law: and if I perish, I perish." Esther's plan resulted in victory!

To obey or disobey is a choice that will produce its own results. Once the right choice is made, then the appropriate action must follow. Pray and ask God for courage and strength to **do the right thing with a made-up mind!**

NEWS FLASH #710

Reflection of the Day:

NEWS FLASH #710

Day 25: Churches Part 1

There is a book of prophecy in the New Testament that speaks of the end time. It introduces us to a day when the glorified Christ will be revealed as the King of eternity. It also gives a promise of blessing for those who hear and heed what the book says. This book is the book of Revelations. It is an unveiling and revealing look at Jesus Christ through His servant, John.

John was "in the spirit on the Lord's day" and was given revelation to write and send letters to the seven churches in Asia. Each church was given personal instructions that would bring about the changes that God required. As you read through these messages to the seven churches, check your heart and life to see what changes you may need to make to prepare for the Lord's soon return.

The church at Ephesus: "The loveless church." They were commended for their work in ministry, patience, and opposition of evil, but, reprimanded because they left their first love. They had drifted from their devotion to Christ. A church can be very active and doctrinally pure and yet have something missing. The Lord admonishes them to remember where they once were spiritually; and to repent and return to their first works.

The Church at Smyrna: "The persecuted church." They were rich in spiritual matters. God knew their faithfulness and hardships. Although there was no promise of relief from suffering, God encouraged them to be not afraid but remain faithful and He would give them a crown of life. "if we suffer, we shall also reign with him."

The church at Pergamos: "The lenient church." It was a thriving church that flourished in the midst of heathen worship. Jesus wanted them to be certain of His provision of salvation when evil runs rampant. They were reprimanded for the doctrine of Balaam and

NEWS FLASH #710

the Nicolaitans. They did not participate in these wrongful acts, but they did not oppose them. God's people must take a stand against anything that will destroy biblical principles. God told them to repent.

These first three churches were told to repent and return to their first love, not to be afraid and to remain faithful, and He would give them a crown of life.

TO BE CONTINUED:

Reflection of the Day:

NEWS FLASH #710

Day 26: Churches Part 2

Jesus was sitting on the Mount of Olives, the very place where the prophet Zechariah predicted the Messiah would stand when He came to establish His kingdom (Zechariah 14:4). Jesus' disciples wanted to know what the sign would be of His coming and the end of the world (Matthew 24:3). He emphasized that they should be less concerned with knowing the exact date and more concerned with being prepared.

The Church at Thyatira: "The compromising church." They were commended for their charity, service, faith, and patience, but reprimanded for permitting a dangerous spirit of Jezebel to be in leadership. God desires that the church be established and maintain definitive boundaries between the church and the world. Jezebel and her children would be destroyed, and the faithful would inherit the kingdom of God.

The Church at Sardis: "The dying church." Admonished to be watchful and strengthen those things that remain, and they were advised to remember where God had brought them from. Remembering brings repentance, and it should be a daily exercise for all of God's people. God told the faithful few that they would walk with Him in white garments. They needed to repent and hear how the Spirit was telling them to live.

The Church at Philadelphia: "The obedient church." They walked hand in hand with God and would share in the blessings of heaven. The Lord promised that they would be kept from the hour of temptation. The Lord Jesus will come and redeem His church. As in all the churches, God knew their works. A person's works reveals the condition of their heart.

NEWS FLASH #710

The Church at Laodicea: "The lukewarm church." This church saw themselves as rich and in need of nothing. God saw them as "wretched, miserable, poor, and blind and naked." God counseled them to buy His everlasting riches, righteousness, and spiritual eye to see what's important and eternal. They were to repent of their lukewarm attitude. God warned the seven churches of needed changes before His return. What changes do you need to make?

NEWS FLASH #710

Reflection of the Day:

Day 27: The Dry Spell Is Over!

In Numbers 13:2 (KJV), we read about the promise of God that has already been given. *"Send thou men, that they may search the land of Canaan, which I give unto the children of Israel: of every tribe of their fathers shall ye send a man, every one a ruler among them."* Now is the time to enter into the promised possessions because, THE DRY SPELL IS OVER!

God has appointed us a **"this time"** blessing. Our part is to believe God and make the necessary preparations to obey His will. Looking at Numbers 13:20-33 (KJV), after returning from searching the land, it was just as God said, *"a land flowing with milk and honey."* As they continued to talk, realizing that fear had entered in, Caleb began to quiet the people telling them, *"let us go up at once, and possess it; for we are well able to overcome it."* But they did not believe and began to give an evil report, *"...we were in our own sight as grasshoppers, and so we were in their sight."*

In Numbers 14:23-24 (KJV) God speaks, *"Surely they shall not see the land which I sware unto their fathers, neither shall any of them that provoked me see it: But my servant Caleb, because he had another spirit with him, and hath followed me fully, him will I bring into the land whereinto he went; and his seed shall possess it."*

Your promised land might be healing in your body. It may be restoration in your marriage or family relationship. Some may desire a building, land or even a business. The fact that someone or something has possession of your 'promised land' does not change the truth that it belongs to you.

Even though you may not see your way because of the giants, keep trusting God as you move forward. When we look to God, everything we need is with Him. Keep on praying and praising,

NEWS FLASH #710

always expecting the victory before you see the manifestation. When we believe and receive instructions from God for the next move or action to take, it is at that time that we declare that "THE DRY SPELL IS OVER."

Reflection of the Day:

Day 28: Say No To Condemnation!

To condemn means to declare to be unfit, evil, or wrong. It pronounces a person to be guilty with a sentence of doom. Because of the redemptive work of Jesus Christ on the cross, every born-again Christian has the right and God given authority to say, **"no to condemnation."**

We find this God given authority in Romans 8:1-2 (KJV), *"There is therefore now no condemnation to them which are in Christ Jesus, who walk not after the flesh, but after the Spirit. For the law of the Spirit of life in Christ Jesus hath made me (put your name here) free from the law of sin and death."* The Spirit of life given to the believer is our freedom from condemnation. Condemnation is the result of bondage and produces spiritual death.

Again in John 3:17 (KJV), we see that God is not the author of condemnation. *"For God sent not his Son into the world to condemn the world; but that the world through him might be saved."* The mission of condemnation comes from the thief, who wants to kill, steal, and destroy you. God sent His son Jesus to give you abundant life.

Another example of condemnation is when the believer misplaces his or her confidence. Hebrews 3:14 (KJV) declares, *"For we are made partakers of Christ, if we hold the beginning of our confidence stedfast unto the end."* Confidence in God is another way of saying **"no to condemnation."**

Our confessions, what we are saying, can bring condemnation. For example, when we say things like, 'nothing good ever happens; I can't; I am a failure,' and on and on. Hebrews 10:35 (KJV), encourages the believer to, *"Cast not away therefore your confidence, which hath great recompense of reward."* To every

Christian, to say what God says about you provides life and eternal rewards.

Trusting in and acting on the word of God is an eliminator of condemnation. God's word lets us know who we are, what we have and what we can do. Whatever you may be dealing with today, search God's truth for your freedom and walk in victory every day when you learn to say, **"NO TO CONDEMNATION!"**

Reflection of the Day:

Day 29: A Sure Foundation

We live in a world with constant changes .. From one stage of life to the next, we experience changes. Some changes work for good; others we might say are a lesson well learned. There is one thing in particular that should remain constant for every child of God. That one thing is the foundation on which we build our lives. When life is full of joy and peace, our foundation doesn't really seem to matter. But when crises come, our foundation is tested. It is during these times that we understand the importance of having a sure foundation.

A foundation is the basis upon which something or someone stands or is supported. It is the base or substructure laid down as a beginning point on which to build. Precise and accurate calculations are required. Jesus is the foundation on which we build our lives. The "Chief Corner Stone" is the most important part.

There are at least two ways to destroy a structure or an individual's life. One is to tamper with the foundation, and another is to build with inferior or substandard materials. Psalms 11:3 (KJV) asks a profound question, *"If the foundation be destroyed, what can the righteous do?"* First, we need to check the foundation. *Therefore whosoever heareth these sayings of mine, and doeth them, I will liken him unto a wise man, which built his house upon a rock:"* (Matthew 7:24 KJV). Practicing obedience to God's word builds a solid foundation. Are you hearing and doing? Could this be the CRACK in your foundation?

Secondly, we need to check the materials. *"If any man's work abide which he hath built thereupon, he shall receive a reward."* (1 Corinthians 3:14) We must build with high-quality materials such as faithfulness, sincerity, honesty, and righteous living. Truth is always timely. Every choice we make for good sets into motion other opportunities for good. Lies, selfishness, and wrong motives are inferior materials that won't stand the test of time. Don't allow achievements, notoriety, or status to cause your building to CRUMBLE. Build your life on a "**SURE FOUNDATION**."

Few Of Us Notice Deterioration After Time It's Our Nomination
When Jesus Christ is not our
Sure Foundation

Reflection of the Day:

Day 30: Get The Word On It!

The Word of God is the way of salvation. It is comfort in times of sorrow and loneliness. The Word of God is relief in times of suffering. It is guidance in times of decision and protection in the times of danger. The Word of God is courage in the times of fear and peace in times of turmoil. It is rest in the times of weariness and strength in times of temptation. The Word of God is a warning in times of indifference and forgiveness in times of conviction.

Psalms 19:7 (KJV) makes it very clear, *"The law of the Lord is perfect, converting the soul: the testimony of the Lord is sure making wise the simple."* The Word of God is a perfect and sure answer to all of life's endeavors.

There are so many benefits made available in the Bible to the heirs of salvation. Knowing that this is true, one might ask, why aren't more people. confessing God's Word and possessing the benefits? One reason could be lack of knowledge. Hosea 4:6 (KJV) says, *"My people are destroyed for lack of knowledge; because thou hast rejected knowledge, I will reject thee, that thou shall be no priest to me: seeing thou hast forgotten the law of God; I will also forget thy children."* Learning and appropriating God's way of doing things produces results. In other words, the Word of God works when you work it.

When we receive God's Word we receive God. When we know God's Word we know God. When we reject God's Word we reject God. Rejecting God's word is dangerous because it opens the door to destruction within families and individuals.

In Jeremiah 9:24 (KJV) it says, *"But let him that glorieth glory in this, that he understandeth and knoweth me, that I am the Lord which exercise loving kindness, judgment, and righteousness in*

the earth: for in these things I delight, saith the LORD." God puts a higher priority on knowing Him personally and living a life that reflects Him. Do you know the God of the Holy Bible? John 1:14 says, *"And the Word was made flesh and dwelt among us..."* Take time with God, while you have time to take.

Reflection of the Day:

NEWS FLASH #710

News Flash # 710 Views & Expressions

For me, the newsletter has provided another avenue and reminder to seek God in all things. Being a quarterly newsletter, #710 arrives as a surprise for me, almost like an unexpected gift in the mail. In 2020 it certainly brought us light into this dark world, and for that we are grateful. We love you Johnny and Pearl.

    -- Minister Meisha & Deacon Michael Senior, Phenix City, AL

Pearl, you and Johnny continue to be a blessing in so many ways. Sharing the good news of the Lord is exactly what the world needs. In the last letter you quoted Psalms 46 "be still and know that I am God". Just think of how many of us are doing just the opposite. We get so busy RUSHING TO DO "This" life that we easily lose focus on the "Giver" of life! Such a necessary word especially in this season! Keep them coming!

    -- Daniel "Thunder" & Kara Turner, Jacksonville FL.

I am grateful for the News Flash #710. It has timely words that speak to my situation and are on point, just what I need. It's encouraging and uplifting words. Explanations are easy to read and understand. Keep it up and look forward to the next issue. Love Patrice

    -- Minister Patrice Mickens, Columbia, SC

News Flash #710 is very inspirational and informative. Eric and I look forward to reading it every time we receive it in the mail. We appreciate you sending the News Flash #710 to us.

    -- Pastor Eric & First Lady Nina Seldon, Upatoi, GA

News Flash #710, the one titled "What's The Rush," was very informative as always. But it was your last paragraph that really stuck with me. It was about being in the present awareness, cherishing the moment and seizing every opportunity given, most of all having a relationship with God for all things. "I will be PRESENT." Thank you, Uncle Johnny and Auntie for your words and encouragement to us all. Kim and I love you guys.

-- Mike & Kim Johnson, Snellville, GA

Poem: Jesus Makes Everything All Right

There are days when I am up and down
and it appears there are no friends around

When I look at the situation and
conclude with observation

Jesus makes everything all right

Even though some days seem dark as night
and the door of deliverance is nowhere in sight

Still Jesus Makes Everything All Right

As we are born and walk through life
It helps to remember no matter your plight

It won't always be OK
by just your might
It's going to take

Jesus to Make It All Right

About the Authors

Pearl and her husband, retired First Sergeant Johnny Williams, are both veterans who served in the United States Armed forces. They both grew up in households that had a dedicated reverence for God. After meeting at Fort Sill, Oklahoma, they were married, and from this union, God blessed them with two beautiful daughters, Cerelia and Jennelle.

Johnny and Pearl are born again, spirit-filled ordained ministers of the gospel of Jesus Christ. In their travels, whether it was Europe, Asia, or Hawaii, they have been the graceful benefactors of the power and goodness of almighty God.

Johnny holds a Bachelor of Arts Degree in Sociology / Criminal Justice, while Pearl has a Masters in Ministerial Education & Evangelism. They are constantly reminded of a note written in the Bible left to them by their Aunt Cora. Those words bring clarity and comfort every time they read them. It says, "To live again, is to love Jesus and obey His words" Amen!

www.ingramcontent.com/pod-product-compliance
Lightning Source LLC
Chambersburg PA
CBHW071506070526
44578CB00001B/462